The INTERNATIONAL DAY OF THE GIRL
Celebrating Girls Around the World

Jessica Dee Humphreys and the Hon. Rona Ambrose Illustrated by Simone Shin

A collection of books that inform
children about the world and inspire
them to be better global citizens

Kids Can Press

For Finn and all the Kensington Rats, with love and full confidence for a future of gender equality – J.D.H.

To my parents and grandparents, who encouraged me to use my voice – R.A.

For Liana — a wonderfully wise and strong girl – S.S.

CitizenKid™ is a trademark of Kids Can Press Ltd.

Text © 2020 Jessica Dee Humphreys
Illustrations © 2020 Simone Shin

Foreword by the Hon. Rona Ambrose

Kids Can Press gratefully acknowledges the financial support of the Government of Ontario, through Ontario Creates; the Ontario Arts Council; the Canada Council for the Arts; and the Government of Canada for our publishing activity.

Published in Canada and the U.S. by Kids Can Press Ltd.
25 Dockside Drive, Toronto, ON M5A 0B5

Kids Can Press is a Corus Entertainment Inc. company

www.kidscanpress.com

The artwork in this book was rendered in acrylic paint and digitally in Photoshop.
The text is set in ITC Bookman.

Designed by Marie Bartholomew

Printed and bound in Buji, Shenzhen, China, in 04/2020 by WKT Company

CM 20 0 9 8 7 6 5 4 3 2 1

MIX
Paper from responsible sources
FSC® C010256

Library and Archives Canada Cataloguing in Publication

Title: The International Day of the Girl : celebrating girls around the world / written by Jessica Dee Humphreys and the Hon. Rona Ambrose ; illustrated by Simone Shin.

Names: Humphreys, Jessica Dee, author. | Ambrose, Rona, author. | Shin, Simone, illustrator.

Series: CitizenKid.

Description: Series statement: CitizenKid

Identifiers: Canadiana 20190113650 | ISBN 9781525300585 (hardcover)

Subjects: LCSH: Girls — Social conditions — Juvenile literature. | LCSH: Women's rights — Juvenile literature. | LCSH: Children's rights — Juvenile literature. | LCSH: Girls — Political activity — Juvenile literature.

Classification: LCC HQ1236 .H86 2020 | DDC j305.23082 — dc23

I'll never forget the group of girls I met at the United Nations. They were from many different countries and many different cultures but they had one goal: to create a global day to celebrate girls' rights.

One of the girls, Fabiola Bongbenuoh from Cameroon, asked me, "Will you help us create a day only for us? A day that celebrates girls?" She inspired me to use my voice to champion the International Day of the Girl through Canada's Parliament and the United Nations General Assembly.

She taught me something very important: if we teach girls about their rights at a young age, they are more likely to exercise them as they grow up.

This book celebrating the International Day of the Girl asks us to think about how we can make the world a place where all girls, no matter where they live, smile confidently when they think of pursuing their dreams. It gives us the knowledge and inspiration to fight for gender equality across borders and cultures. These stories are based on the experiences of many girls worldwide who found their voices and changed their lives and their communities for the better. They are our superstars.

I have one question for you: Will you help? Let's use these stories to teach our daughters and sons, girls and boys, about the importance of gender equality and girls' rights. Let's work together so every day is a Day of the Girl.

— *the Hon. Rona Ambrose*

Imagine a garden, growing right in the middle of your town.

One half of the garden is lush and healthy. It gets all the sunshine and water and attention that it needs to thrive.

The other half is wilted and faded. The neighborhood dogs have dug holes, harming the roots and seeds. Careless visitors have trampled the seedlings and sprouts. Passersby plucked blossoms, preventing fruit from growing. And sometimes people sprayed chemicals on the plants, mistaking them for weeds.

But what happens if the entire garden is allowed to flourish and reach its full potential? The neglected half will be able to catch up and grow strong and healthy, too!

Just as gardens need to be nurtured so that they can thrive on their own, so do people. But for a long time, half the children of the world — the girls — have been treated unfairly, often denied the same schooling, freedom, safety and care given to boys.

In 2011, a group of girls from around the world were invited to the United Nations (UN) in New York City, where they gave voice to the issues affecting girls — and only girls — in their communities.

Moved to take action, world leaders agreed that one way to help cultivate gender equality — giving girls and boys equal opportunities and care — would be to create a special day to focus on solving problems that affect girls in particular. For this reason, every October 11, we now celebrate the International Day of the Girl Child.

The millions of girls who inspired this important day also helped inspire the characters and stories in this book. Their experiences remind us how even the youngest of us can overcome challenges and make positive change in our communities and beyond — *every* day.

This is Flora. She is strong.

On her way home from school, Flora often passes a group of boys in the town square practicing a traditional martial art called capoeira [ca-poh-AY-ra]. In their bright white uniforms with colorful cords tied around their waists, they kick and spin in time to rhythms set by music. It looks like fun, and Flora's impressed by their powerful dance-like movements. She watches them for weeks, until she has the courage to ask if she can join.

The instructor leading the class is happy to include her. He knows that learning capoeira can help Flora protect herself when she walks alone on the long, unsafe road to and from school. Men often follow girls there and try to hurt or rob them, thinking they are weak.

"Not anymore!" decides Flora. She trains hard and becomes stronger every day. Slowly, she graduates from level to level, trading her uniform's plain cord for a blue one, then brown and then a green cord. Yellow, purple and red ... Flora keeps progressing.

Flora plans to earn a white cord one day, the highest level a person can achieve. And she looks forward to the day when she can teach capoeira to other young girls in her community so they, too, will have fun while learning how to stay safe.

While Flora's story is set in the large South American country of Brazil, the unfortunate truth is that girls all around the world are at a high risk of violence. Men and boys must be responsible for their own behavior, and everyone — men and women, boys and girls — can work together to stop gender-based violence. One way is to encourage girls to participate in martial arts and sports, which helps them develop valuable physical skills and confidence, and changes attitudes by bringing girls and boys together as friends and teammates.

This is Hana. She is smart.

Hana loves books and spends every moment she can reading. She can't imagine what life would be like if she hadn't learned to read. And that could have easily happened.

For 20 years, girls in Hana's country were forbidden to attend school. Her mother had not been allowed an education, and neither had Hana. But Hana was lucky because her grandmother had taught her to read … in secret.

Each morning, Hana's grandmother and her friends had gathered at a different house, bringing their granddaughters along. They pretended to be simply drinking tea and chatting, but really the women were teaching the girls how to read and write. These grandmothers believed their granddaughters had as much right to learn as their grandsons.

Finally, the law changed, and Hana and her friends were at last allowed to go to school! Although they sit on the dusty ground in tattered tents while the nearby boys' school has proper classrooms, all the girls are excited to be learning. Hana is looking forward to becoming a teacher and giving other girls the gift of literacy, just as her grandmother gave her.

Around the world, millions of girls do not attend school. Sometimes, this is because their families can't afford school fees or live too far from a school. Other times — as happened in Afghanistan where Hana's story takes place — it is because schooling for girls is forbidden by law or by custom. This is bad not only for the girls but for everyone around them. When girls are educated, they have the tools to create a better future for themselves, their families and their communities.

This is Abuya. She is creative.

Abuya always enjoys watching her father work, so one day she asks him to teach her woodworking, too. He shows her how to use his tools safely, and together they make a box to hold spices for her mother, and a toy for her baby brother. Abuya is proud of what she made, but now she wants to build something even more useful.

One morning, Abuya overhears her older sister asking to stay home from school. She explains that her friends often miss their classes because there are no toilets at the high school. Students must use a nearby ditch or stream when they need to go, which makes the girls feel unsafe.

"Aha!" thinks Abuya, who now knows what her next project should be.

With the help of her father and his carpenters' guild, Abuya and her friends learn the basics of carpentry — measuring, sawing and hammering. Within weeks, they all know enough to begin their project.

The walls of the outhouse they build are sturdy and provide the students with much-needed privacy. Everyone is pleased, especially Abuya, who can now look forward to high school and to becoming a carpenter when she grows up.

In rural areas of Kenya, and in many other countries around the world, up to half of the schools do not have basic toilet facilities. Without proper toilets, there is a lack of privacy which can be embarrassing, as well as unsanitary and unsafe. As a result, many girls stop attending school. When washroom facilities are provided, girls are more likely to attend school regularly and get the education they deserve.

This is Liliya. She is inventive.

Liliya lives on the outskirts of a big city near a dark tunnel and an open water canal, where the paths are rough and broken. It is a dangerous place, especially for girls. Strangers often lurk in the tunnel, and Liliya and her friends are told to stay away for their safety.

Because she isn't allowed to go out on her own very often, Liliya spends lots of time on her computer. While Liliya plays a game one day, her character is chased into the water by monsters that had been hiding in a cave. Suddenly, it occurs to her that some of the dangers in the game are like those in her own community.

Using the game to make a model of her neighborhood, Liliya crafts solutions to the problems. She places lights in the tunnel to make sure no one can hide there. She builds a solid fence along the canal so no one can fall in. And she lays a smooth path that everyone can use.

At her parents' suggestion, an excited Liliya presents her ideas to the city council, which has been looking for ways to make improvements. Within a few months, a plan is approved. Liliya and the other girls in her community look forward to being able to roam as freely in their real neighborhood as Liliya does in her virtual world.

Worldwide, children with disabilities are especially at risk of violence and abuse. But girls with disabilities face even further discrimination — they are much more often excluded from health care and public education, and are less likely to have their opinions heard. For a child like Liliya — living in a remote area of a vast country like Russia — computers are one way to learn useful skills while staying connected with others and forming their own virtual communities.

This is Sokanon. She is brave.

Sokanon's community does not have a proper school. Instead, she and the other students sit in cold and moldy temporary classrooms in trailers that were originally meant to be used as portable washrooms. Sokanon knows this isn't healthy, and it isn't fair. She decides to do something about it.

The leaders of her community help Sokanon spread her message to thousands of schoolchildren across the country, whom she asks to write letters to the government. And when the letters don't work, Sokanon gives speeches in front of thousands of grown-ups, demanding a new school. And when *that* doesn't work, she *still* doesn't give up.

Sokanon is frustrated to discover that many adults don't take her seriously simply because she is a girl. But she believes that *because* she is a girl, and an Indigenous person, her voice is important and needs to be heard. So she perseveres, meeting with important people in the government, speaking from the heart and continuing to push for what she knows is right.

Eventually, thanks to Sokanon's leadership, hard work and willingness to speak out, the government agrees to provide the money needed to build the school. The children of Sokanon's community can finally look forward to having a safe and comfortable place to learn.

Girls' opinions are often ignored, particularly by large organizations such as governments. This is especially true for girls from Indigenous communities, such as the Attawapiskat First Nation in northern Canada where Sokanon's story is set. When girls' voices aren't heard, it affects how they see themselves and what they believe they can do and become. For example, of the almost 200 countries in the world, fewer than 20 are led by women. Changing this situation starts with encouraging girls to speak up and with decision-makers valuing their contributions.

This is Mallika. She is talented.

Mallika helps cook the family meals every morning, noon and night, and makes spicy *dal* even tastier than her mother's. She is proud to be trusted to make fancy treats on special occasions.

Yet there often isn't much food for Mallika herself to eat, because it is the tradition in her house for female family members to eat only after the men and boys have finished. On many days, Mallika feels tired and weak, so eventually her worried mother takes her to the doctor. The doctor explains that Mallika is suffering from anemia, a health problem caused by a lack of proper nutrition.

That night, her parents hold a family meeting so they can all discuss the problem and decide what to do.

Her brothers are the first to speak up. "I'm sorry, Mallika!" cries Kamal. "It's unfair we get to take more than you," agrees Neeraj. "I guess it's just the way we've always done it," says Mallika. "Change takes time," admits her father. "But we will make a start right now," says her mother with a smile. They agree to eat their meals all together, with everyone getting a fair share.

To celebrate, Mallika makes her favorite dessert for the whole family to enjoy ... together.

In parts of India, as well as in many other countries, girls are twice as likely to suffer from malnutrition than boys, and one in every three girls is anemic. This is often the result of a traditional practice in which women and girls eat only after the male family members have finished. When families cannot afford to buy more food, sharing equally sometimes means some people will get less to ensure that others get more. This can be a difficult idea for some to accept, but the fact is that equality benefits everyone in the end.

This is Keeya. She is caring.

Keeya loves babies — baby animals, baby birds and most of all her baby sister! But she doesn't want a baby of her own right now. She'd rather go to school, play with her friends and just … be a kid! Keeya's older sister was married when she was 11 years old and had two babies by the time she was 14. Keeya worries that this will be expected of her, too.

So with the help of her teacher, Keeya researches the many ways early marriage is harmful for girls. She learns that it prevents them from going to school, separates them from their friends and family, and endangers their health if they have babies too young. Next, Keeya borrows a video camera donated to her school. She interviews her sister about what it's like to be a wife and mother so young, and makes a film explaining her research.

Keeya presents her film to the religious leaders and decision-makers of her village and waits nervously as weeks go by. After much discussion and debate sparked by Keeya's film, the community eventually agrees to outlaw child marriage. Overjoyed by the news, Keeya hugs and kisses her baby sister. She feels as free as a bird.

Throughout the world — in countries as different as Nigeria, India and Brazil — millions of girls are expected, and sometimes even forced, to marry. But education is key to ending the practice of child marriage. When a girl completes her schooling, it is far more likely that her future income will be higher, she will wait until she is an adult to decide about marriage, and any children she has will be healthier — as she will be, too.

This is Zarah. She is funny.

Sadly, there is little to joke about when a war forces Zarah's family and millions of others to leave their city. After a long and difficult journey, Zarah and her family arrive at a hot and crowded refugee camp.

Natural disasters and conflicts are dangerous for everyone, but girls can be especially affected. In wars like the one in Zarah's home country of Syria, girls are twice as likely to be harmed as boys. And girls in refugee camps are much less likely to attend school, because of the potential for gender-based violence, as well as gender discrimination. Living with this kind of isolation and constant fear can take a terrible toll on a girl's mental health. Laughter and play are important to the mental well-being of children in disaster situations, so much so that the United Nations Convention on the Rights of the Child specifically states that every child has the right to play.

On their first day, Zarah tries to fetch water for the family, but she is shoved out of the long line by angry men who shout rude things at her to frighten and embarrass her. When she tells her parents what happened, they forbid her to leave the tent alone. The camp is a dangerous place for young girls on their own.

As the days pass, Zarah notices other girls in nearby tents. She can see they are angry, scared and bored, just as she is. There is no school to go to. There are no books to read. There is no music, no internet, no TV. And no laughter.

"Enough of this!" thinks Zarah. She calls to the girls nearby and tells them her best jokes. It feels so good to laugh. She asks the girls to tell the jokes to their brothers, who are allowed outside. The boys then pass on the jokes to children they meet, who in turn tell them to *their* families. Her plan works! The jokes spread throughout the camp, and the shared laughter makes Zarah and the other girls feel less alone and a little more normal while they wait to return home one day.

This is Aster. She is ambitious.

Aster loves outer space and has visited the planetarium on every birthday she can remember. She made a model solar system to hang above her bed when she was in kindergarten. Over the years, she has taken out every book the library has on planets, stars and galaxies. And each night, she dreams about flying through the universe as an astronaut.

However, Aster notices that most characters on her favorite science TV shows are boys. "Weird," thinks Aster. She also realizes a lot of the toys and books about outer space are placed in an area of the local store marked, *For Boys*. "Super weird," she thinks.

When she asks her parents if science isn't for girls also, they tell her about some of the brilliant women scientists who have made huge contributions to space travel, such as NASA mathematician Katherine Johnson, cosmonaut Valentina Tereshkova and astrophysicist Jocelyn Bell Burnell.

Inspired, Aster starts an after-school club for anyone interested in learning about astronomy. She's surprised by the number of kids — boys and girls — who join! The club meets every week, and they call themselves the Asteroids, in honor of their club's founder.

Girls and boys do equally well in science, technology, engineering and math (STEM) subjects, but a recent study found that many girls in the United States, where Aster lives, "believe" that they are not as good at math as boys. This has an influence on the quality of education they receive and the subjects they choose to study. Worldwide, only 3 percent of students in information and communication technology are female; the percentage is similar in math (5 percent) and in engineering (8 percent). Encouraging girls to enter science, technology, engineering and math (STEM) fields ensures equality and diversity in these important professions.

You Are the World's Gardener!

If we think of the whole world as a garden, then *you* are one of its gardeners. Plant seeds of change! Feed the ideas you want to grow! Prop each other up and don't cut one another down! Reach high and take up space! Raise your voice! Cultivate fairness and harvest equality!

Girl children everywhere continue to face discrimination specifically because of their gender. But by celebrating the International Day of the Girl Child, we are celebrating girls from all over the world who are facing their challenges with strength, intelligence, creativity, imagination, bravery, skill, kindness, humor and ambition. On October 11 you, too, can join all the children and adults who are working hard to make the world a safer and more equal place.

From Seed to Fruition:

A Timeline of How the International Day of the Girl Came to Be

Each year since 2012, the nations of the world have celebrated a special day that brings attention to the needs of and challenges facing girls. The International Day of the Girl reminds countries, organizations and individuals to address those needs and focus on those challenges, while promoting girls' empowerment and ensuring the fulfillment of their human rights. But it was a very long time coming! Here is a timeline that traces the hard work by many people over many years that finally made this important day a reality.

1945:
The United Nations (UN) forms with an aim to ensure that all countries of the world work together to prevent war. Member nations discuss problems that affect the entire world and agree on solutions. Right from the start, the UN recognizes that women and men are equals; however, children's rights are not mentioned.

1954:
The UN creates Universal Children's Day, celebrated every November 20, to promote the welfare of children worldwide.

1959:
The UN chooses Universal Children's Day to adopt the Declaration on the Rights of the Child, a document recognizing that children are different from adults and so require special care and protection.

2011:

Girl delegates from seven different countries are chosen by Plan International to attend the UN Commission on the Status of Women. In a meeting with Canada's then Minister for the Status of Women, the Hon. Rona Ambrose, they describe their personal struggles and accomplishments, and ask her to take up the cause of establishing a day just for girls.

2011:

Minister Ambrose returns to Canada with the difficult mission of convincing her government to formally request an International Day of the Girl at the UN. She joins forces with women from all the political parties and finally persuades the entire parliament to agree.

2009:

Plan International Canada's "Because I'm a Girl" campaign launches an online petition asking the UN to establish a special day focusing on issues particular to girls: the International Day of the Girl.

2011:

Minister Ambrose addresses the entire United Nations: "We will never know the secret struggles that millions of young girls across the world fight and lose every day to break the barriers they face in health, in education and in the challenges of everyday life. I have met some of these girls … and I have been moved by what they had to say." She continues, "An International Day of the Girl would help raise awareness of these struggles and help these young girls improve their lives, the lives of their communities, their villages, their towns and maybe their countries."

1989:

The UN adopts the Convention on the Rights of the Child. This treaty describes the rights that every child has, including the right to **protection from harm**, the right to an **education**, the right to a **safe environment**, the right to **play** and the right to **participate in making decisions that affect them**. However, it does not recognize that girls face additional, unique challenges.

2011:

Finally, it is confirmed: October 11 officially becomes the International Day of the Girl!

Further Information About Some Issues Facing Girls

The statistics behind the stories in this book are difficult to read, but they are important to know if we are to work together to change them.

Gender-Based Violence

• One out of every three women worldwide has experienced some form of violence in their lives. *(Source: World Health Organization, 2017. https://www.who.int/news-room/fact-sheets/detail/violence-against-women.)*

• Every 10 minutes, a girl somewhere in the world dies as a result of violence. *(Source: United Nations Population Fund, 2016. https://www.unfpa.org/news/power-10-ten-astonishing-facts-about-10-year-old-girls.)*

Illiteracy

• Although around the globe youth literacy rates are rising, there are still parts of the world where women and girls significantly lag behind. *(Source: UNICEF, 2019. https://data.unicef.org/topic/education/literacy/.)*

• In countries where overall literacy rates are still very low, as few as one in four women can read. *(Source: UNICEF, 2019. https://data.unicef.org/topic/education/literacy/.)*

Computer Literacy and Internet Access

• A study found that 30 percent of girls aged 11 to 16 believe "computing is more for boys." *(Source: Girlguiding UK, 2017. https://www.girlguiding.org.uk/globalassets/docs-and-resources/research-and-campaigns/girls-attitudes-survey-2017.pdf.)*

• Globally, millions fewer women and girls have access to the internet than men and boys. *(Source: Measuring Digital Development, ITU Publications, 2019. https://www.itu.int/en/ITU-D/Statistics/Documents/facts/FactsFigures2019.pdf.)*

Disability

• Girls and women with any form of disability are among the more vulnerable and marginalized of society. *(Source: Women with Disabilities Fact Sheet, United Nations Economic and Social Council. https://www.un.org/development/desa/disabilities/resources/women-with-disabilities-fact-sheet.html.)*

• Globally, women and girls make up three-quarters of the disabled people in low- and middle-income countries. Between 65 percent and 70 percent of these women live in rural areas where health and education resources are already difficult to access. *(Source: "Making the SDGs Count for Women and Girls with Disabilities." UN Women, 2019. https://www.un.org/development/desa/disabilities/wp-content/uploads/sites/15/2019/10/Making-SDGs-count-for-women-with-disabilities.pdf.)*

Access to Education

• Globally, over 130 million girls do not attend school. *(Source: UNICEF. https://www.unicef.org/education/girls-education.)*

• The main barriers to girls' education include poverty and the lack of money to pay school fees; expectations that girls should perform domestic chores instead of attending school; early marriage and pregnancy; long distances to schools make walking potentially unsafe; fear of gender-based violence at school; and lack of girls' bathrooms at schools. *(Source: PLAN Canada. https://plancanada.ca/girls-education.)*

Sanitation

• A major barrier to girls' education is the lack of access to girls-only washrooms. *(Source: "11 Lessons about Water, Sanitation, and Hygiene in Schools." UNICEF, 2018. https://www.unicef.org/stories/11-lessons-water-school.)*

• In rural areas throughout Africa, South America and South Asia, as many as half the schools do not have basic toilet facilities. *(Source: Drinking water, Sanitation and Hygiene in Schools: Global Baseline Report. WHO/UNICEF, 2018. https://www.unicef.org/media/47671/file/JMP-WASH-in-Schools-ENG.pdf.)*

Advocacy and Decision-Making

• Girls are currently the largest "excluded group" in the world, meaning they are the most overlooked in the development of international, national and local laws and protections. *(Source: "Building a Platform for Girls Rights." Plan International, 2018. https://plan-international.org/blog/2018/02/building-platform-girls-rights.)*

• When bias in the classroom means male students are given more opportunities to speak than girls, it creates long-term negative effects on girls and the careers they eventually choose. *(Source: "On the Origins of Gender Human Capital Gaps: Short-and Long-Term Consequences of Teachers' Stereotypical Biases" by Victor Lavy and Edith Sand. American National Bureau of Economic Research, 2015. https://www.nber.org/papers/w20909.)*

Nutrition

• In many low- and middle-income countries, girls are twice as likely than boys to suffer from malnutrition, and one in every three girls is anemic. *(Source: Canada's Feminist International Assistance Policy, Global Affairs Canada, 2017. https://www.international.gc.ca/world-monde/assets/pdfs/iap2-eng.pdf?ga=2.255095104.991512909.1575502626-568288754.1574692303.)*

• In many societies globally, women and girls eat only after male family members, resulting in undernutrition. *(Source: Food and Agriculture Organization of the United Nations (FAO), http://www.fao.org/3/al184e/al184e00.pdf.)*

Child Marriage

• In the least-developed nations, 12 percent of girls are married before the age of 15. *(Source: "Child Marriage." United Nations Population Fund (UNFPA). https://www.unfpa.org/child-marriage.)*

• Each year, approximately 15 million girls as young as 10 are married. *(Source: "Child Marriage Around the World." UNICEF, 2019. https://www.unicef.org/stories/child-marriage-around-world.)*

Emergencies and Natural Disasters

• More than three-quarters of the world's refugees and displaced persons are women and girls. *(Source: "'EmPOWER' girls before, during and after crises, UN says on International Day of the Girl Child." United Nations Refugees and Migrants, 2017. https://refugeesmigrants.un.org/empower-girls-during-and-after-crises-un-says-international-day-girl-child.)*

• In times of crisis, girls are two and a half times more likely to be out of school than boys. *(Source: "27 Million Children Out of School in Conflict Zones." UNICEF Fact Sheet, 2017. https://www.unicef.org/media/media_100857.html.)*

Gender Representation in Science, Technology, Engineering and Mathematics (STEM)

• Women are less likely than men to graduate in fields related to science and engineering, and the proportion of women graduating in STEM fields remains low in both poor and rich countries. *(Source: "The World's Women 2015: Trends and Statistics." United Nations Department of Economic and Social Affairs, 2015. https://unstats.un.org/unsd/gender/downloads/worldswomen2015_report.pdf.)*

• Women are underrepresented in science fields in every region of the world. Today, only 30 percent of all of the world's researchers are women. *(Source: "Just 30% of the world's researchers are women. What's the situation in your country?" UNESCO eAtlas of Research and Experimental Development. https://en.unesco.org/news/just-30-world%E2%80%99s-researchers-are-women-whats-situation-your-country.)*

Acknowledgments

The stories in this book are based on my interviews and research into real girls' experiences from all around the globe. Thanks to the following organizations for sharing information about their work with girls that helped to inspire these stories:

Through the **Block by Block Foundation**, Mojang (the makers of the video game *Minecraft*), Microsoft and UN-Habitat (the UN program for sustainable cities) collaborate on an innovative program in which *Minecraft* is used to involve the community in the design of urban public spaces. **www.blockbyblock.org**

The **First Nations Child & Family Caring Society of Canada** provides research, policy, professional development and networking to support First Nations child and family services agencies caring for First Nations children, youth and families. An important project of the Caring Society is Shannen's Dream, a youth-focused social justice campaign in honor of Shannen Koostachin, a girl youth education advocate from Attawapiskat First Nation. **www.fncaringsociety.com**

Plan International Canada is a development and humanitarian organization that advances children's rights and equality for girls all over the world. Plan International Canada was the primary leader in the movement to create the UN International Day of the Girl Child. **www.plan-international.org** and **plancanada.ca**

Studio Samuel works to empower at-risk girls in Africa to become self-reliant and steers them away from the barriers that are all too common among those living in poverty, including child marriage and lack of access to education. Studio Samuel's Training for Tomorrow program provides life-skills training to vulnerable young women in Ethiopia. **www.studiosamuel.org**

With deep thanks for their essential insights and inspiration: Cindy Blackstock, Fabiola Bongbenuoh, Kimberly Davis, Gabby Frierson, Yvette Ghione, Guy Hamel, Kathryn and Savannah Harding, Emily Hillstrom, Helga Holland, Tamara Horton of Studio Samuel, Serena Koostachin, Ilana Landsberg-Lewis, Christine Martins of Axé Capoeira, Emma Russell-Trione, Joanne Sandler, Brock Shepherd, Findley Shepherd -Humphreys, Birtukan Shiferaw, Avielle Specter-Bloch, Sophie Thompson, Pontus Westerberg of UN-Habitat and Larissa Zaharuk. Special gratitude to Meghan Francis and her team at Plan International Canada, as well as Alana Kapell and Stacey Roderick, for their many invaluable contributions to this book. — J.D.H.

Without the dedication and commitment of so many people from many parts of the Canadian government and across all political parties in the Canadian parliament, the International Day of the Girl would not have happened. Thank you to Roseline MacAngus; Ambassador Guillermo Rishchynski; the Hon. Lawrence Cannon; Suzanne Clément; Sébastien Goupil; Suzanne Cooper; Gitane De Silva; all of the Canadian Members of Parliament, in particular MP Hedy Fry, MP Irene Mathyssen and MP Maria Mourani; UN Under Secretary General Michelle Bachelet; and Emily Hillstrom. To my husband, JP Veitch, and our children, Makena and Garrison, who were there from the first UN resolution to the celebration of the first #dayofthegirl! — R.A.